DINACHAR

The Ayurvedic Morni
Using Ancient Ayurveda Lifestyle Wisdom to Set up Your
Day for Health and Happiness!

INGRID HAMILTON

Copyright © 2017

Table of Contents

Contents

How This Book Can Help You:

It seems to me like there is an ever increasing fascination with morning routines and the habits people have when they start their day. More and more people are watching online videos to see videos on how people spend their mornings or listening to podcasts to learn more about what successful people do in the morning. I personally think this obsession comes from the knowing that how you start your day is fundamental to how the rest of your day goes and people are looking for ideas on healthy habits that they can incorporate in their morning routine to set things up for success.

I truly believe that having healthy habits in the morning can make you healthier, more physically fit, and more successful because good habits are the foundation of all of those things and there is no better time to implement them than in the morning. Now, when I decided to look into morning routines more myself, I came across the Dinacharya which is the Ayurvedic version of a morning and or daily routine. I became facinated with both the process and reasoning of why they completed the things they did in the morning for a healthy and happy life.

I wanted to write a book on it because I feel these habits could be so beneficial for people to learn about and incorporate into their daily lives. I understand that doing all these items on a daily basis may not be practical for most people but I wanted to write about them individualy so people could choose what they most want to do and what works best for them. Do the habits in the order that works best for you.

WHAT IS DINACHARYA AND AYURVEDA?

Ayurveda was developed more than 3,000 years ago in India. Ayur stands for life and Veda stands for science or knowledge. Ayurveda is one of the world's oldest holistic medical systems that is still existence today. It is based on a philosophy that to treat one thing you need to have a balance between mind, body, and spirit. Once you bring the body into balance it can then heal itself.

Ayurveda also has the philosophy that everyone's individual nature is mirrored in their body type or dosha. There are three main dosha types that people can be called Vata (air), Pitta (fire) and Kapha (earth-water). Each person can also have a combination of the three types but each one has their own set of protocols and practices that is best for the individual depending on what type they are. I am not going to go into all the different characteristics of the three different types in this book as that is a whole book. I recommend you do some research to find out which type you are most predominantly as it will help you with picking the best practices for you in this book.

Dinacharya is an Ayurvedic term for daily practice. Dina means daily and Charya means routine or regimen. The Dinacharya really embodies the art of self-care. Practicing the Dinacharya is about taking in the cycles of nature when creating routine and establishing balance. The purpose of the Dinacharya is to maintain physical health and happiness through body, mind and spirit. It is also about cleansing the body from built up toxins and awakening the senses so you are ready to start your day.

CHAPTER 1. IMPORTANCE OF WAKE TIME

Everyone has heard the saying the early bird catches the worm but in Ayurveda how early you wake up really depends on your dosha or personal constitution.

They say that everyone should wake up before sunrise which depends on season but that the following wake times should be used for the following doshas:

Vata – 6:00 a.m.

Pitta – 5:30 a.m.

Kapha – 4:30 a.m.

The philosophy with these wake times is that there is a natural ebb and flow within the natural world that depending on your own individual constitution, your body responds best to different times of the day for performing individual activities.

Within the Dinacharya it is also important to spend a few minutes after you wake up in gratitude or prayer followed by setting your intention for the day to come.

This allows you to remember what is important in life and set your day on a positive note.

Chapter 2. Oil Pulling

You may or may not have already heard about oil pulling as it is becoming more and more popular in modern day use. Oil pulling is an ancient Ayurvedic practice, also referred to as oil gargling, based on the philosophy that when you wake up your mouth has accumulated a lot of toxins also known as ama that your body needs to get rid of. They feel the most powerful way to do this is by swishing oil in your mouth for 5-20 minutes. The oil then binds to the bacteria, toxins, plaque, and even stains on your teeth. Once you spit out the mixture you not only have fresher breath, but overtime can whiten teeth.

There are other claimed benefits to oil pulling besides fresher breath and whiter teeth. It is said to help detox the body, increase energy, help keep skin clear, strengthen gums and jaw, prevent cavities, boost immune system, and reduce inflammation. Whether or not you believe in these claimed benefits, oil pulling will drastically help you reduce your morning breath and is worth doing for that reason alone. Look at it as a natural very effective mouthwash that does not have all the chemicals and toxins that traditional mouthwash does.

How to oil pull:

To oil pull you only need about a teaspoon or two of oil to swish around in your mouth. The most popular oils are coconut, sesame (not toasted), and sunflower. Olive oil will also work. Once you put the oil in your mouth you continuously swish around for a minimum of five minutes and not to exceed 20 minutes pulling it in and out of between your teeth in the process. Although plenty of sources suggest you need to do it for the full 20 minutes, you only need to do it for 5-10 minutes to see full results. You are supposed to do it first thing in the morning, on an empty stomach. I recommend you do it as soon as you wake up in the morning by keeping some by your bed. That way it keeps you from swallowing all the toxins and bacteria that have built up in your mouth while sleeping. Once you are done, spit it in the trash. Never spit the oil in the sink because it can clog pipes. I like to do it as I am just getting out of bed and stretching for the day. I also like to make a custom oil mixture with a mixture of half coconut oil and half sunflower oil. I keep it in a small glass bottle next to my bed and add a few drops of peppermint essential oil. The reason I like this mixture is because both coconut oil and sunflower oil when combined have a pretty neutral taste. Coconut oil is the all-star when it comes to oil pulling because it is naturally antibacterial and antimicrobial. The one problem with it is that it stays solid at colder temperatures and can be harder to work with unless you use a new spoon daily. If you mix it though with around 50% of another oil, like sunflower, it will stay in its liquid form.

I highly suggest you give oil pulling a try. It is super easy to incorporate into your morning routine, as you can do it while still doing other things. It is now something I look forward to doing every morning and have a hard time going without.

CHAPTER 3. CLEANSING THE SENSES - EYES

After you are done oil pulling in the morning and have spit the oil in the trash, it is time to start cleansing the senses.

Starting with eyes the first thing you want to do is splash your face with cool water and massage the eyes by gently rubbing them. Complete this process by doing an eyewash using one of the following procedures:

One of the simplest ways to wash your eyes is simply splashing with water, but the following are the traditional Ayurvedic practices used for an eyewash.

Rosewater is a very popular and traditional eyewash in Ayurveda. To wash eyes, fill an eyewash cup ½ full with high quality, organic, additive free rose water and the other half with warm (not hot) purified water. Rose water is also known as hydrosol and there are versions you can make yourself, just make sure you use organic roses. Then lift your head/eye cup upward as you tilt your head back, allowing the diluted rose water to fill the eye cavity of your closed eye. Then open your eye and soak your eye in the rose water for a few moments, blinking a few times. Be sure that you're not wearing eye makeup when you do this.

As an alternative, use triphala eye wash. Triphala is an herbal blend of haritaki, bibhitaki and amalaki. To make triphala eye wash: add ½ teaspoon of triphala powder to a glass or ceramic cup and add 8 ounces boiled, filtered water. Stir the triphala and hot water mixture well, remove the spoon, and leave it to cool. It's suggested to make this in the evening and leave it overnight for morning use. Alternatively, make it in the morning and leave it all day for evening use. An hour is usually long enough for all of the sediment to be well settled and the solution to become saturated with triphala's beneficial nutrients. Strain with cheesecloth and use as described above.

Chapter 4. Cleansing the Senses - Mouth

After your eyes are clean it is time to start on oral care. These are things that can be done in addition to oil pulling to assure healthy teeth and gums.

The first part of cleansing the mouth in an Ayurvedic oral care practice is to scrape the tongue. Tongue scraping, although very popular today and recommended by dentists, is another one of those things that started with Ayurveda. The purpose of tongue scraping is to remove the film that you see covering your tongue in the morning. Ayurveda refers to it as built up ama, and they say it can compromise your digestive and immune system. The purpose of tongue scraping is to remove that toxic coating before it gets reabsorbed by the body. You scrape your tongue by using a tongue scraper made from stainless steel, sterling silver, or copper. Start by relaxing your tongue, then place the scraper as far back on your tongue as possible and slowly scrape your tongue while moving the tool forward. Rinse, then repeat a few times until your tongue looks clean and pinkish or red in color.

Another popular oral care practice in Ayurveda is to chew on black sesame seeds. They are believed to help polish the teeth and remove stains while providing the teeth with much needed minerals.

Last but not least, make sure you use a natural, toxin-free herbal toothpaste or powder to brush your teeth. Ones containing neem are very popular in Ayurveda. Rinsing and gargling with warm salt water is another way to keep the mouth and throat healthy and alkalized.

CHAPTER 5. CLEANSING THE SENSES - NOSE

The most effective way to cleanse your nose is doing a nasal rinse using what is known as a Neti Pot. This helps to clean out debris, pollutants, and allergens to keep your sinuses and nasal passages clean. This may not be something you want to do daily and can just do it when you feel your nasal passages could benefit from being cleaned out.

It is very easy to perform using a ceramic Neti Pot. Put in ¼ teaspoon of sea salt or pharmaceutical grade salt (do not use table salt). Next, boil some distilled water (do not use tap water for this). Pour the Neti Pot about half full with boiling water and let the salt dissolve. Fill the rest of the way with the cooler distilled water so that the mixture is room temperature. Standing in the shower, or over the bathroom sink, place the spout of the Neti Pot in one nostril and tip your head to the opposite side. The saline water enters one nostril from the spout of the pot, and exits the other nostril, having traveled through and cleansed the nasal passages by the gentle force of gravity. Do the other side by placing the spout of the Neti Pot in your other nostril and tipping your head the other way. Do the other side by placing the spout of the Neti Pot in your other nostril and tipping your head the other way.

Another popular way of cleansing the nasal passages in Ayurveda is to use nasya Oil. nasya oil is an herbal infused oil that you can either make yourself with recipes online or purchase. In place of nasya oil you could also just use sesame oil (untoasted) or ghee, which is clarified butter.

To administer, place a drop of nasya oil on your little finger and gently insert into nostril. Gently massage the inner walls of your nose and then alternate to the other nostril.

There are many claimed benefits to doing this including helping with hoarseness of voice and stiffness of the head along with assisting with things like greater clarity of mind and a calmer nervous system. The main benefit of nasya is to lubricate dry nasal passages which can help prevent things like nose bleeds. It can also help with immunity and is good to do before certain actives like flying in an airplane.

CHAPTER 6. CLEANSING THE SENSES - EARS

The final way to cleanse the senses is to clean out the ears. Now just a reminder, some of these things like cleaning the eyes, nose, and ears do not need to be done on a daily basis and may be best done when you most feel like you need them.

Cleaning ears the Ayurvedic way, also known as Karna Purana, can help with conditions such as ringing in the ears, excess ear wax, poor hearing, headaches, and TMJ.

To clean your ears, start by warming an oil like sesame, ghee, or an herbal oil made specifically for ear cleaning. Then, apply a few drops of oil to each ear and massage into the ear lobe and bones. Repeat on the other side. Also, close the ear flap and using medium pressure gently massage the ear canal by pressing the ear flap in a circular motion. If there is any pain, stop and seek the help of a medical professional.

CHAPTER 7. WARM WATER AND ELIMINATION

Now that your senses are cleansed, it is time to start cleansing yourself internally. The traditional way to do this is to drink a warm or hot cup of lemon water. Lemon water is known to help stimulate the bowels in the morning to help with effective elimination. Elimination is considered an important part of the Ayurvedic routine in the morning.

Other benefits of lemon water include stimulating digestion, flushing out toxins, stimulating weight loss, helping keep the body alkaline and providing a healthy dose of vitamin C along with other beneficial minerals.

There are other ingredients that you can add to your lemon water to help give the drink even more healing benefits. These include raw honey, ginger, turmeric, cayenne, sea salt, and ghee. Now you probably do not want to add all of these at once, but each of them has their own benefits individually that you could research to see which ones work best for you. You can also choose to swap out lemon with lime if you prefer.

The most important part of this ritual is to drink the hot or warm water upon waking it is very stimulating and nurturing to the body and helps to get the body moving when you drink it first thing. It is a good idea to rinse your mouth with some warm salt water when you are done to keep the acid in the lemon from harming the enamel on your teeth.

CHAPTER 8. EXERCISE AND YOGA

Regular exercise has a lot of benefits. It increases energy, improves circulation, keeps you fit and healthy, and aids in weight loss. Yoga includes all those benefits but is also a way to stay centered and get additional piece of mind in the morning.

Whatever workout you choose, it is important to get some daily yoga into your Dinacharya practice. In Ayurveda you want to customize your workout and yoga routine depending on your dosha. The following are some examples of what might be best depending on your dosha type.

Kapha – Kapha body type does best with fast aerobic exercise done vigorously. The best yoga moves in the morning for Kapha are sun salutation done twelve times rapidly then move onto the Bridge, Peacock, Palm Tree, and Lion.

Vata – Vata body types do best with slow and gentle exercise. Yoga is a great one but anything else that focuses on show movements other ones to consider are walking at a slow pace or Tai Chi. The best yoga moves in the morning for Vata are sun salutations done twelve times slowly, then move onto Camel, Cobra, Cat, and Cow.

Pitta – Pita body types do best with moderate exercise. Some examples include, fast paced walks, swimming and bicycle riding as long as it is not too intense. The best yoga moves in the morning for pita are doing moon salutations 16 times at a moderate pace then move onto Fish, Boat, and Bow pose.

CHAPTER 9. ABHYANGA – SELF MASSAGE

Ok now for the best part of your morning doing a self-massage. Abhyanga, which is considered a form of Ayurvedic medicine and an important part of a daily Dinacharya, involves a massage of the body using large amounts of warmed oil.

Doing Abhyanga provides many benefits including nourishing the body and decreasing the effects of aging, lubricating the joints, increasing circulation, stimulating the internal organs, assisting in elimination of impurities, moving the lymph fluid, calming the nerves, and smoothing the skin. Even if you can't do it daily, it is good to aim for 2-4 times a week. The best oils to use for Abhyanga are coconut, sesame, or sunflower. Jojoba, almond, and olive oil work well too. It is good to aim for oils that will balance your dosha.

To do Abhyanga, warm the oil. I like to do so by placing a small glass bottle of oil into a cup of hot water. Then start by applying oil to the crown of your head and massaging your scalp. Massage your face and ear lobes in and upward movement. Use long strokes on your legs and arms and circular strokes on your joints. Always massage toward the direction of your heart. Massage your abdomen in clockwise circular motions. Finish by completing a foot massage. You are going to want to have the oil sit on you for 5-15 minutes before bathing which is a good time to start on the next activities.

CHAPTER 10. PRANAYAMA AND MEDITATION

Now that you are all lubed up with oil, it is a good time to do the following practices while you are waiting for the oil to be absorbed into your body.

Pranayama is the formal practice of controlling the breath. Breath is considered in Ayurveda to be prana and prana is considered a vital life force. The benefits of doing Prana are that it calms the mind, improves focus and attention, increases energy, and boosts the immune system.

One of the most popular pranayama breathing exercises is to sit cross-legged. Close the right nostril with your right thumb and inhale deeply through the left. Close your left nostril with your ring finger as you release the right. Exhale slowly through your right nostril. Repeat the process at least ten times alternating between the nostrils.

After you have finished your breathing exercises, it is a good time to do some meditation. Meditation, as you are probably already aware, has many benefits including reducing stress, increasing happiness, and improving concentration. There are many different types of meditation you can try out including Zen, Mantra, Vipassana, and Transcendental. It is important to research and pick the one that will work best for you. For a very simple meditation just sit cross-legged for 5-20 minutes while focusing on your breath.

CHAPTER 11. BATHING

After you have oiled yourself up and had time to let it absorb by doing breathing exercises and meditation, it is time to jump into the bath or shower, depending on your preferences.

Ayurveda sees bathing as a therapeutic activity. It is therefore considered and important part of your Dinacharya, or daily routine.

Ancient Ayurvedic texts speak of therapeutic baths featuring rose petals, milk, honey, and different spices.

Ayurvedic texts report the many benefits of a healing bath including; enhancing physical energy levels while improving mental clarity and removing sweat, dirt, and environmental toxins from the skin. It also relaxes the mind and balances the emotions.

It is important in Ayurveda when bathing to use products that will not strip your skin and are non-toxic. They tend to use more natural products when bathing and do not use traditional soap on the skin as it tends to strip it of its natural oils and acid mantle which are used to protect the skin_. They also tend to use essential oils when bathing for and aromatherapy experience.

Because they do not use traditional soap, a very popular cleanser in Ayurveda is called ubtan. Usually they use gram flower and mix it with either sandalwood powder or turmeric. They also usually add milk to make a paste or a milk powder and add water. There are lots of different ubtan recipes online, so find the one that you think will work best.

CHAPTER 12. BREAKFAST AND REST OF DAY

Now that you have completed all the steps in your daily Dinacharya, it is time to have breakfast and continue with the rest of your day.

Ayurveda stresses the importance of fruit in the morning, usually cooked. A balancing Ayurvedic breakfast usually consists of stewed apples, pears, and dates stirred into hot cereal and then cooked with some warming spices. Warming spices include things like pepper, cardamom, cayenne, cinnamon, cloves, turmeric, and fresh ginger. You can also add some ghee, honey, or high-quality milk to the dish. It is also very important in Ayurveda to be mindful when eating and to chew slowly.

After breakfast, it is time to get dressed and go about the rest of your day. At this point your mind, body, and spirit should be completely nourished by following this routine.

I hope you enjoyed this book on Dinacharya the Ayurvedic morning routine. Although it may not be practical to do all these things every day, pick a few that resonate most with you to get in the practice of doing them regularly. Then you can add more in when you have more time or feel a particular practice will be beneficial. Wishing you many wonderful mornings to come on your journey to a healthier and happier you.

Namaste.

Notes:

Notes:

Notes:

About The Author

Ingrid Hamilton enjoys nature, reading, and writing. She is an animal lover with three birds and two cats which she shares her beautiful home with. Ingrid really loves using ancient wisdom to teach people how to live happier and healthier lives and hopes to inspire people to go back to a more natural way of living.

One Last Thing:

If you enjoyed this book or found it useful I'd be very grateful if you'd post a short review on Amazon. Your support really does make a difference and I read all the reviews personally so I can get your feedback and make this book even better.

Thanks again for your support!

Made in the USA
Coppell, TX
07 May 2020